DOUBLING
Circus Stars

Based on the Math Monsters™ public television series,
developed in cooperation with the National Council
of Teachers of Mathematics (NCTM).

by John Burstein

Reading consultant: Susan Nations, M.Ed., author/literacy coach/consultant
Math curriculum consultants: Marti Wolfe, M.Ed., teacher/presenter; Kristi Hardi-Gilson, B.A., teacher/presenter

WEEKLY WR READER®
EARLY LEARNING LIBRARY

Please visit our web site at: **www.earlyliteracy.cc**
For a free color catalog describing Weekly Reader® Early Learning Library's list
of high-quality books, call 1-877-445-5824 (USA) or 1-800-387-3178 (Canada).
Weekly Reader® Early Learning Library's fax: (414) 336-0164.

Library of Congress Cataloging-in-Publication Data

Burstein, John.
    Doubling: circus stars / by John Burstein.
      p. cm. — (Math monsters)
      Summary: The four Math Monsters demonstrate the concept of doubling
at the Double Fun Circus.
      ISBN 0-8368-3807-6 (lib. bdg.)
      ISBN 0-8368-3822-X (softcover)
      1. Multiplication—Juvenile literature. [1. Multiplication.] I. Title.
QA115.B964   2003
513.2'13—dc21
                                       2003045007

This edition first published in 2004 by
Weekly Reader® Early Learning Library
330 West Olive Street, Suite 100
Milwaukee, WI 53212 USA

Original Math Monsters™ animation: Destiny Images
Art direction, cover design, and page layout: Tammy Gruenewald
Editor: JoAnn Early Macken

Printed in the United States of America

1 2 3 4 5 6 7 8 9 07 06 05 04 03

You can enrich children's mathematical experience by working with
them as they tackle the Corner Questions in this book. Create
a special notebook for recording their mathematical ideas.

Doubles and Math

Children in primary grades learn to combine numbers. Working with
doubles demonstrates an excellent mental math strategy
to help them accomplish this task.

Meet the Math Monsters™

ADDISON

Addison thinks
math is fun.
"I solve problems
one by one."

MINA

Mina flies
from here to there.
"I look for answers
everywhere."

MULTIPLEX

Multiplex
sure loves to laugh.
"Both my heads
have fun with math."

Split is friendly
as can be.
"If you need help,
then count on me."

SPLIT

We're glad you want to take a look
at the story in our book.

We know that as you read, you'll see
just how helpful math can be.

Let's get started. Jump right in!
Turn the page, and let's begin!

The Double Fun Circus came to Monster Town.
The band marched along. They sang,
"The Double Fun Circus is coming your way!
The Double Fun Circus is coming today!"
The Math Monsters wanted to join in the fun.

"I will juggle," said Addison.

"I will do magic," said Mina.

"I will be a strongman," said Multiplex.

"I will watch and cheer," said Split.

What are some things you might see at a circus?

Addison went first. He tossed a ball from hand to hand.

"I will juggle with one ball," he said. "Then I will double that."

"Now I am juggling two balls," he said. "I won't stop there. I will double the balls again."

How many balls will Addison juggle next?

Before their very eyes, Addison juggled four balls.
Split clapped and cheered.

"If you double four balls, how many will that make?"
asked Multiplex.

"Eight!" puffed Addison as he juggled them all.

"Can you double them again?" asked Split.

How many balls will Addison juggle now?

"I have sixteen balls in the air," said Addison.

"If you double sixteen, you will have thirty-two!" said Mina.

"I cannot juggle that many," said Addison. "I will stop and rest."

Multiplex took his turn.

"I will lift this bar," he said. "I have five pounds on one side. I have five pounds on the other side."

If Multiplex lifts the bar with five pounds on each side, how many pounds will he lift in all?

"I am lifting ten pounds," said Multiplex.
"I can do more."

Mina added one pound to the left side. Addison added one pound to the right side.

"Wow! Six pounds on each side!" said Multiplex.

If Multiplex lifts the bar, how many pounds will he lift?

"I am lifting twelve pounds," said Multiplex.
Split clapped. She said, "You are very strong."
"Thank you," said Multiplex. "I can lift more."

Addison added one more pound
to the right side.

Mina added one more pound to
the left side.

"Now I have seven pounds
on each side," said Multiplex.

*How many pounds
will Multiplex
lift now?*

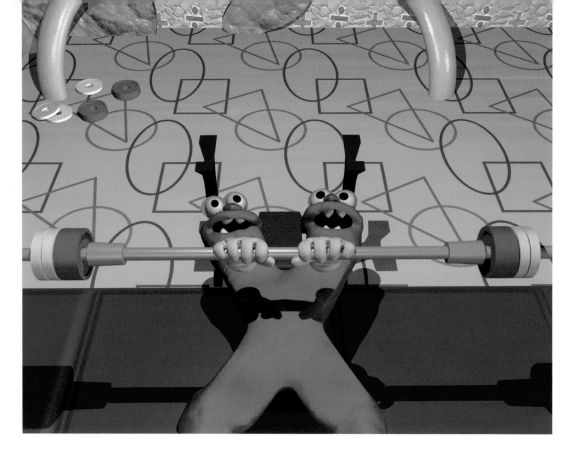

"Seven and seven make fourteen pounds," said
Multiplex. "I can still lift more."

"There is no more time," said Split. "Mina is going to
start her magic act."

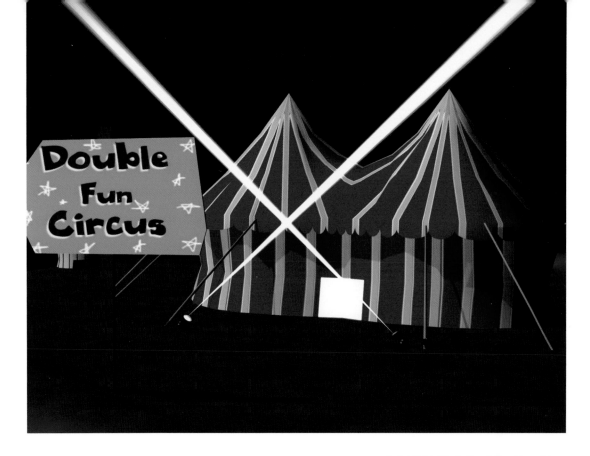

The monsters ran to the big circus tent. They went inside.

What do you think the monsters will see in the tent?

Mina came out to do her magic act.

"I have five birds and a magic hat," said Mina.

"Whatever goes into the hat will be doubled."

Magic Mina
and her
Magic Doubling Hat

Mina told her five birds to fly into the hat. Then she said her magic rhyme.

"Magic hat, magic hat, double that, double that."

If Mina's magic works, how many birds will fly out of the hat?

19

Ten birds flew out of the hat!
The monsters cheered.
"Do it again," said Split.

Ten birds flew into the hat.
Mina said her magic rhyme.
"Magic hat, magic hat,
double that, double that."

*How many birds
will fly out of the
hat this time?*

21

Twenty birds flew out of Mina's hat!
The monsters clapped and clapped.

Multiplex sang,
"Two and two are four.
Four and four are eight.
The Double Fun Circus
is really great!
Double the fun
makes everyone cheer.
Can the Triple Fun Circus
come to town next year?"

*What does
Multiplex mean?
How is triple
different than
double?*

ACTIVITIES

Page 5 Using children's prior knowledge of the circus, help them identify how math can be used in a variety of circus contexts, such as counting the number of clowns coming out of a car, measuring how high the tightrope is, or figuring out how much food to buy the animals.

Pages 7, 9, 19, 21 Young children need to use everyday objects to practice, apply, and understand abstract mathematical concepts. Create some circus acts of your own. Try using small objects such as beans, pennies, or blocks to represent Addison's juggling balls or Mina's birds. Help children re-create the monsters' doubling acts.

Pages 11, 13, 15 Make your own small model of a teeter-totter by balancing a pencil lengthwise on a narrow bowl or drawing a large picture of a balance scale on a piece of paper. Use small, equal-sized objects such as beans or paper clips to simulate Multiplex's barbell. Act out these problems and explore different ways to balance the scale by keeping an equal number of objects on both sides. Stay in the children's comfort zone during these exercises.

Page 17 Role-play a doubling circus act children might perform based on Addison's or Multiplex's circus act.

Page 23 Using a variety of everyday objects, such as those listed above, explore the difference between doubling and tripling numbers.